Perfect
Love

PERFECT LOVE

The Meditations, Prayers, and Writings

of

Teresa of Ávila

—⚬—

Edited by
Trace Murphy

IMAGE BOOKS
DOUBLEDAY
NEW YORK LONDON TORONTO SYDNEY AUCKLAND

AN IMAGE BOOK
PUBLISHED BY DOUBLEDAY
a division of Bantam Doubleday Dell Publishing Group, Inc.
1540 Broadway, New York, New York 10036

IMAGE, DOUBLEDAY, and the portrayal of a deer drinking
from a stream are trademarks of Doubleday, a division of
Bantam Doubleday Dell Publishing Group, Inc.

First Image Books edition published November 1995

Grateful acknowledgment is made to Sheed & Ward for
permission to reprint excerpts from translations by
E. Allison Peers.

Library of Congress Cataloging-in-Publication Data
Teresa, of Avila, Saint, 1515–1582.
Perfect love : the meditations, prayers, and writings of
Teresa of Avila / edited by Trace Murphy.
p. cm.
''An Image book.''
1. Meditations. 2. Spiritual life—Catholic Church.
3. Catholic Church—Doctrines. I. Murphy, Trace. II. Title.
BX2179.T3E5   1995   95–34821
248.4'82—dc20   CIP

ISBN 0-385-48049-0

Contents

III

The Interior Castle 87

IV

Maxims 141

PART I

The Life of Teresa of Jesus

The first draft of The Life of Teresa of Jesus, the first of the three major works written by Teresa, was completed in June of 1562 when she was forty-seven. Like many of her writings, it is a spiritual autobiography in the tradition of Augustine's Confessions. In the first selection here, Chapter 1, Teresa talks about her early life, her family, and how she lost her mother when she was still very young. In Chapter 4 she tells how she came to decide on a life as a nun, and how at this stage she experienced many challenges in her health and her spiritual life. Later in the Life, Teresa offers guidance for prayer and uses the image of water to teach her method for conversation with God. In Chapter 18 she describes the fourth water, and gives encouragement to practitioners to use prayer in striving for the highest states in union with God here on earth.

Chapter 1

If I had not been so wicked it would have been a help to me that I had parents who were virtuous and feared God, and also that the Lord granted me his favor to make me good. My father was fond of reading good books and had some in Spanish so that his children might read them too. These books, together with the care which my mother took to make us say our prayers and to lead us to be devoted to Our Lady and to certain saints, began to awaken good desires in me when I was, I suppose, about six or seven years old. It was a help to me that I never saw my parents inclined to anything but virtue. They themselves had many virtues. My father was a man of great charity toward the poor, who was good to the sick and also to his servants—so much so that he could never be brought to keep slaves, because of his compassion for them. On one occasion, when he had a slave of a brother of his in the house, he was as good to her as to his own children. He used to say that it caused him intolerable distress that she was not free. He was strictly truthful; nobody ever heard him swear or speak evil. He was a man of the most rigid chastity.

My mother, too, was a very virtuous woman, who endured a life of great infirmity; she was also particularly chaste. Though extremely beautiful, she was never known to give any reason for supposing that she made the slightest account of her beauty; and, though she died at thirty-three, her dress was already that of a person advanced in years. She was a very tranquil woman, of great intelligence. Throughout her life she endured great trials and her death was most Christian.

We were three sisters and nine brothers; all of them, by the goodness of God, resembled their parents in virtue, except myself, though I was my father's favorite. And, before I began to offend God, I think there was some reason for this, for it grieves me whenever I remember what good inclinations the Lord had given me and how little I profited by them. My brothers and sisters never hindered me from serving God in any way.

I had one brother almost of my own age. It was he whom I most loved, though I had a great affection for them all, as had they for me. We used to read the lives of saints together; and, when I read of the martyrdoms suffered by saintly women for God's sake, I used to think they had purchased the fruition of God very cheaply; and I had a keen desire to die as they had done, not out of any love for God of which I was conscious, but in order to attain as quickly as possible to the fruition of the great blessings which, as I read, were laid up in heaven. I used to discuss with this brother of mine how we could become martyrs. We agreed to go off to the country of the Moors, begging our bread for the love of God, so that they might behead us there; and, even at so tender an age, I believe the Lord had given us sufficient courage for this, if we could have found a way to do it; but our greatest hindrance seemed to be that we had a father and a mother. It used to cause us great astonishment when we were told that both pain and glory would last forever. We would spend long periods talking about this and we liked to repeat again and again, "Forever—ever—ever!" Through our frequent repetition of these words, it pleased the Lord that in my earliest years I should receive a lasting impression of the way of truth.

When I saw that it was impossible for me to go to any place where they would put me to death for God's sake, we decided to become hermits, and we used to build hermitages, as well as we could, in an orchard which we had at home. We would make heaps of small stones, but they at once fell down again, so we found no way of accomplishing our desires. But even now it gives me a feeling of devotion to remember how early God granted me what I lost by my own fault.

I gave alms as I could, which was but little. I tried to be alone when I said my prayers, and there were many such, in particular the rosary, to which my mother had a great devotion, and this made us devoted to them too. Whenever I played with other little girls, I used to love building convents and pretending that we were nuns; and I think I wanted to be a nun, though not so much as the other things I have described.

I remember that, when my mother died, I was twelve years of age or a little less. When I began to realize what I had lost, I went in my distress to an image of Our Lady and with many tears besought her to be a mother to me. Though I did this in my simplicity, I believe it was of some avail to me; for whenever I have commended myself to this sovereign virgin I have been conscious of her aid; and eventually she has brought me back to herself. It grieves me now when I observe and reflect how I did not keep sincerely to the good desires which I had begun.

O my Lord, since it seems thou art determined on my salvation—and may it please thy majesty to save me!—and on granting me all the graces thou hast bestowed on me already, why has it not seemed well to thee, not for my advantage but for thy honor, that this habitation wherein thou hast had continually to dwell should not have become so greatly defiled? It grieves me, Lord, even to say this, since I know that the fault has been mine alone, for I believe there is nothing more thou couldst have done, even from this early age, to make me wholly thine. Nor, if I should feel inclined to complain of my parents, could I do so, for I saw nothing in them but every kind of good and anxiety for my welfare. But as I ceased to be a child and began to become aware of the natural graces which the Lord had given me, and which were said to be many, instead of giving him thanks for them, as I should, I started to make use of them to offend him.

Chapter 4

During this time, when I was considering these resolutions, I had persuaded one of my brothers, by talking to him about the vanity of the world, to become a friar, and we agreed to set out together, very early one morning, for the convent where that friend of mine lived of whom I was so fond. In making my final decision, I had already resolved that I would go to any other convent in which I thought I could serve God better or which my father might wish me to enter, for by now I was concerned chiefly with the good of my soul and cared nothing for my comfort. I remember—and I really believe this is true—

that when I left my father's house my distress was so great that I do not think it will be greater when I die. It seemed to me as if every bone in my body were being wrenched asunder; for, as I had no love of God to subdue my love for my father and kinsfolk, everything was such a strain to me that, if the Lord had not helped me, no reflections of my own would have sufficed to keep me true to my purpose. But the Lord gave me courage to fight against myself and so I carried out my intention.

When I took the habit, the Lord at once showed me how great are his favors to those who use force with themselves in his service. No one realized that I had gone through all this; they all thought I had acted out of sheer desire. At the time my entrance into this new life gave me a joy so great that it has never failed me even to this day, and God converted the aridity of my soul into the deepest tenderness. Everything connected with the religious life caused me delight; and it is a fact that sometimes, when I was spending time in sweeping floors which I had previously spent on my own indulgence and adornment, and realized that I was now free from all those things, there came to me a new joy, which amazed me, for I could not understand whence it arose. Whenever I recall this, there is nothing, however hard, which I would hesitate to undertake if it were proposed to me. For I know now, by experience of many kinds, that if I strengthen my purpose by resolving to do a thing for God's sake alone, it is his will that, from the very beginning, my soul shall be afraid, so that my merit may be the greater; and if I achieve my resolve, the greater my fear has been, the greater will be my reward, and the greater, too, will be my retrospective pleasure. Even in this life his majesty rewards such an act in ways that can be understood only by one who has enjoyed them. This I know by experience, as I have said, in many very serious matters; and so, if I were a person who had to advise others, I would never recommend anyone, when a good inspiration comes to him again and again, to hesitate to put it into practice because of fear; for, if one lives a life of detachment for God's sake alone, there is no reason to be afraid that things will turn out amiss, since he is all-powerful. May he be blessed forever. Amen.

• • • •

The change in my life, and in my diet, affected my health; and, though my happiness was great, it was not sufficient to cure me. My fainting fits began to increase in number and I suffered so much from heart trouble that everyone who saw me was alarmed. I also had many other ailments. I spent my first year, therefore, in a very poor state of health, though I do not think I offended God very much during that time. My condition became so serious—for I hardly ever seemed to be fully conscious, and sometimes I lost consciousness altogether—that my father made great efforts to find me a cure. As our own doctors could suggest none, he arranged for me to be taken to a place where they had a great reputation for curing other kinds of illness and said they could also cure mine. This friend whom I have spoken of as being in the house, and who was one of the seniors among the sisters, went with me. In the house where I was a nun, we did not have to make a vow of enclosure. I was there for nearly a year, and during three months of that time I suffered the greatest tortures from the drastic remedies which they applied to me. I do not know how I managed to endure them; and in fact, though I did endure them, my constitution was unable to stand them, as I shall explain. My treatment was to commence at the beginning of the summer and I had left the convent when the winter began. All the intervening time I spent in the house of the sister whom I referred to above as living in a village, waiting for the month of April, which was near at hand, so that I should not have to go and come back again.

On the way there, I stopped at the house of this uncle of mine, which, as I have said, was on the road, and he gave me a book called *Third Alphabet,* which treats of the Prayer of Recollection. During this first year I had been reading good books (I no longer wanted to read any others, for I now realized what harm they had done me) but I did not know how to practice prayer, or how to recollect myself, and so I was delighted with the book and determined to follow that way of prayer with all my might. As by now the Lord had granted me the gift of tears, and I liked reading, I began to spend periods in solitude, to go frequently to confession and to start upon the way of prayer with this book for my guide. For I found no other guide (no confessor, I mean) who understood me, though I sought one for fully twenty years subsequently to the time I am speaking of. This did me great harm, as I had frequent relapses, and might have been completely lost; a guide would at least have helped me to escape when I found myself running the risk of offending God.

In these early days his majesty began to grant me so many favors that at the end of this entire period of solitude, which lasted for almost nine months, although I was not so free from offending God as the book said one should be, I passed over that, for such great care seemed to me almost impossible. I was particular about not committing mortal sin—and would to God I had always been so! But about venial sins I troubled very little and it was this which brought about my fall. Still, the Lord began to be so gracious to me on this way of prayer that he granted me the favor of leading me to the Prayer of Quiet, and occasionally even to Union, though I did not understand what either of these was, or how highly they were to be valued. Had I understood this I think it would have been a great blessing. It is true that my experience of Union lasted only a short time; I am not sure that it can have been for as long as an *Ave Maria;* but the results of it were so considerable, and lasted for so long that, although at this time I was not twenty years old, I seemed to have trampled the world beneath my feet, and I remember that I used to pity those who still clung to it, even in things that were lawful. I used to try to think of Jesus Christ, our good and our Lord, as present within me, and it was in this way that I prayed. If I thought about any incident in his life, I would imagine it inwardly, though I liked principally to read good books, and this constituted the whole of my recreation. For God had not given me talents for reasoning with the understanding or for making good use of the imagination; my imagination is so poor that, even when I thought about the Lord's humanity, or tried to imagine it to myself, as I was in the habit of doing, I never succeeded. And although, if they persevere, people may attain more quickly to contemplation by following this method of not laboring with the understanding, it is a very troublesome and painful process. For if the will has nothing to employ it and love has no present object with which to busy itself, the soul finds itself without either support or occupation, its solitude and aridity cause it great distress and its thoughts involve it in the severest conflict.

People in this condition need greater purity of conscience than those who can labor with the understanding. For anyone meditating on the nature of the world, on his duties to God, on God's great sufferings and on what he himself is giving to him who loves him, will find in his meditations instructions for defending himself against his thoughts and against perils and occasions of sin. Anyone unable to make use of this method is in much greater danger and should occupy himself frequently in reading, since he cannot find instruction in any other way. And inability to do this is so very painful that, if the master who is directing him forbids him to read and thus find help for recollection, reading is nonetheless necessary for him, however little it may be, as a substitute for the mental prayer which he is unable to practice. I mean that if he is compelled to spend a great deal of time in prayer without this aid it will be impossible for him to persist in it for long, and if he does so it will endanger his health, since it is a very painful process.

I believe now that it was through the Lord's good providence that I found no one to teach me; for, had I done so, it would have been impossible, I think, for me to persevere during the eighteen years for which I had to bear this trial and these great aridities, due, as I say, to my being unable to meditate. During all these years, except after communicating, I never dared begin to pray without a book; my soul was as much afraid to engage in prayer without one as if it were having to go and fight against a host of enemies. With this help, which was a companionship to me and a shield with which I could parry the blows of my many thoughts, I felt comforted. For it was not usual with me to suffer from aridity; this only came when I had no book, whereupon my soul would at once become disturbed and my thoughts would begin to wander. As soon as I started to read they began to collect themselves and the book acted like a bait to my soul. Often the mere fact that I had it by me was sufficient. Sometimes I read a little, sometimes a great deal, according to the favor which the Lord showed me. It seemed to me, in these early stages of which I am speaking, that, provided I had books and could be alone, there was no risk of my being deprived of that great blessing; and I believe that, by the help of God, this would have been the case if at the beginning I had had a master or some other person to advise me how to flee from occasions of sin, and, if I fell before them, to get me quickly free from them. If at that time the devil had attacked me openly, I believe I should never in any way have begun to sin grievously again. But he was so subtle, and I was so weak, that all my resolutions were of little profit to me, though, in the days when I served God, they became very profitable indeed, in that they enabled me to bear the terrible infirmities which came to me with the great patience given me by his majesty.

I have often reflected with amazement upon God's great goodness and my soul has delighted in the thought of his great magnificence and mercy. May he be blessed for all this, for it has become clear to me that, even in this life, he has not failed to reward me for any of my good desires. However wretched and imperfect my good works have been, this Lord of mine has been improving them, perfecting them and making them of greater worth, and yet hiding my evil deeds and my sins as soon as they have been committed. He has even allowed the eyes of those who have seen them to be blind to them and he blots them from their memory. He gilds my faults and makes some virtue of mine to shine forth in splendor; yet it was he himself who gave it me and almost forced me to possess it.

Chapter 18

May the Lord teach me words in which to say something about the fourth water. His help is very necessary, even more so than it was for describing the last water, for in that state the soul still feels that it is not completely dead—and we may use this word in speaking of it, since it is dead to the world. As I said, it retains sufficient sense to realize that it is in the world and to be conscious of its loneliness, and it makes use of exterior things for the expression of its feelings, even if this is only possible by signs. In the whole of the prayer already described, and in each of its stages, the gardener is responsible for part of the labor; although in these later stages the labor is accompanied by such bliss and consolation that the soul's desire would be never to abandon it; the labor is felt to be, not labor at all, but bliss. In this state of prayer to which we have now come, there is no feeling, but only rejoicing, unaccompanied by any understanding of the thing in which the soul is rejoicing. It realizes that it is rejoicing in some good thing, in which are comprised all good things at once, but it cannot comprehend this good thing. In this rejoicing all the senses are occupied, so that none of them is free or able to act in any way, either outwardly or inwardly. Previously, as I have said, they were permitted to give some indication of the great joy that they feel; but in this state the soul's rejoicing is beyond comparison greater, and yet can be much less effectively expressed, because there is no power left in the body, neither has the soul any power, to communicate its rejoicing. At such a time everything would be a great hindrance and torment to it and a disturbance of its rest; so I assert that, if there is union of all the faculties, the soul cannot communicate the fact, even if it so desires (when actually experiencing it, I mean); if it can communicate it, then it is not union.

The way in which this that we call union comes, and the nature of it, I do not know how to explain. It is described in mystical theology, but I am unable to use the proper terms, and I cannot understand what is meant by "mind" or how this differs from "soul" or "spirit." They all seem the same to me, though the soul sometimes issues from itself, like a fire that is burning and has become wholly flame, and sometimes this fire increases with great force. This flame rises very high above the fire, but that does not make it a different thing; it is the same flame which is in the fire.

This, with all your learning, your reverences will understand; there is nothing more that I can say of it.

What I do seek to explain is the feelings of the soul when it is in this divine union. It is quite clear what union is—two different things becoming one. O my Lord, how good thou art! Blessed be thou forever! Let all things praise thee, my God, who hast so loved us that we can truly say that thou hast communication with souls even in this exile; even if they are good, this is great bounty and magnanimity. In a word, my Lord, it is a bounty and a magnanimity which are all thine own, for thou givest according to thine own nature. O infinite bounty, how magnificent are thy works! Even one whose understanding is not occupied with things of the earth is amazed at being unable to understand such truths. Dost thou, then, grant these sovereign favors to souls who have so greatly offended

thee? Truly my own understanding is overwhelmed by this, and when I begin to think
about it I can make no progress. What
progress, indeed, is there to be made which
is not a turning back? As for giving thee
thanks for such great favors, there is no
way of doing it, though sometimes I find it
a help to utter foolishness.

• • • •

I propose also to speak of the graces and
effects which remain in the soul, and of
what it can do by itself, if it can do anything, toward reaching a state of such
sublimity.

This elevation of the spirit, or union, is
wont to come with heavenly love; but, as I
understand it, the union itself is a different
thing from the elevation which takes place
in this same union. Anyone who has not
had experience of the latter will think it is
not so; but my own view is that, even
though they may both be the same, the

Lord works differently in them, so that the soul's growth in detachment from creatures is much greater in the flight of the spirit. It has become quite clear to me that this is a special grace, though, as I say, both may be, or may appear to be, the same; a small fire is as much fire as is a large one and yet the difference between the two is evident. In a small fire, a long time elapses before a small piece of iron can become red-hot; but if the fire be a large one, the piece of iron, though it may also be larger, seems to lose all its properties very quickly. So it is, I think, with these two kinds of favor from the Lord. Anyone who has attained to raptures will, I know, understand it well. If he has not experienced it, it will seem ridiculous to him, as well it may be; for a person like myself to speak of such a thing and to make any attempt to explain a matter which cannot even begin to be described in words may very well be ridiculous.

But I believe that the Lord will help me in this, since his majesty knows that, next to doing what I am bidden, my chief aim is to cause souls to covet so sublime a blessing. I shall say nothing of which I have not myself had abundant experience. The fact is, when I began to write about this fourth water, it seemed to me more impossible to say anything about it than to talk Greek—and indeed it is a most difficult matter. So I laid it aside and went to communion. Blessed be the Lord, who thus helps the ignorant! O virtue of obedience, that canst do all things! God enlightened my understanding, sometimes giving me words and sometimes showing me how I was to use them, for, as in dealing with the last kind of prayer, his majesty seems to be pleased to say what I have neither the power nor the learning to express. What I am saying is the whole truth; and thus, if I say anything good, the teaching comes from him, while what is bad, of course, comes from that sea of evil—myself. And so I say, if there are any persons (and there must be many) who have attained to the experiences in prayer which the Lord has granted to this miserable woman, and who think that they have strayed from the path and wish to discuss these matters with me, the Lord will help his servant to present his truth.

Speaking now of this rain which comes from heaven to fill and saturate the whole of this garden with an abundance of water, we can see how much rest the gardener would be able to have if the Lord never ceased to send it whenever it was necessary. And if there were no winter, but eternal warm weather, there would never be a dearth of flowers and fruit and we can imagine how delighted he would be. But during this life, that is impossible, and, when one kind of water fails, we must always be thinking about obtaining another.

This rain from heaven often comes when the gardener is least expecting it. Yet it is true that at first it almost always comes after long mental prayer; as one degree of prayer succeeds another, the Lord takes this little bird and puts it into the nest where it may repose. Having watched it flying for a long time, striving with mind and will and all its strength to seek and please God, it becomes his pleasure, while it is still in this life, to give it its reward. And what a great reward that is! For even a moment of it suffices to recompense the soul for all the trials that it can possibly have endured.

While seeking God in this way, the soul becomes conscious that it is fainting almost completely away, in a kind of swoon, with an exceeding great and sweet delight. It gradually ceases to breathe and all its bodily strength begins to fail it; it cannot even move its hands without great pain; its eyes involuntarily close, or, if they remain open, they can hardly see. If a person in this state attempts to read, he is unable to spell out a single letter; it is as much as he can do to recognize one. He sees that letters are there, but, as the understanding gives him no help, he cannot read them even if he so wishes. He can hear, but he cannot understand what he hears. He can apprehend nothing with the senses, which only hinder his soul's joy and thus harm rather than help him. It is futile for him to attempt to speak; his mind cannot manage to form a single word, nor, if it could, would he have the strength to pronounce it. For in this condition all outward strength vanishes, while the strength of the soul increases so that it may the better have fruition of its bliss. The outward joy experienced is great and most clearly recognized.

This prayer, for however long it may last, does no harm; at least, it has never done any to me, nor do I ever remember feeling any ill effects after the Lord has granted me this favor, however unwell I may have been; indeed, I am generally much the better for it. What harm can possibly be done by so great a blessing? The outward effects are so noteworthy that there can be no doubt some great thing has taken place; we experience a loss of strength but the experience is one of such delight that afterward our strength grows greater.

It is true that at first this happens in such a short space of time—so, at least, it was with me—that because of its rapidity it can be detected neither by these outward signs nor by the failure of the senses. But the exceeding abundance of the favors granted to the soul clearly indicates how bright has been the sun that has shone upon it and has thus caused the soul to melt away. And let it be observed that, in my opinion, whatever may be the length of the period during which all the faculties of the soul are in this state of suspension, it is a very short one; if it were to last for half an hour, that would be a long time—I do not think it has ever lasted so long as that with me. As the soul is not conscious of it, its duration is really very difficult to estimate, so I will merely say that it is never very long before one of the faculties becomes active again. It is the will that maintains the contact with God but the other two faculties soon begin to importune it once more. The will, however, is calm, so they become suspended once again; but eventually, after another short period of suspension, they come back to life.

With all this happening, the time spent in prayer may last, and does last, for some hours; for, once the two faculties have begun to grow inebriated with the taste of this divine wine, they are very ready to lose themselves in order to gain the more, and so they keep company with the will and all three rejoice together. But this state in which they are completely lost, and have no power of imagining anything—for the imagination, I believe, is also completely lost—is, as I say, of brief duration, although the faculties do not recover to such an extent as not to be for some hours, as it were, in disorder, God, from time to time, gathering them once more to himself.

Let us now come to the most intimate part of what the soul experiences in this condition. The persons who must speak of it are those who know it, for it cannot be understood, still less described. As I was about to write of this (I had just communicated and had been experiencing this very prayer of which I am writing), I was wondering what it is the soul does during that time, when the Lord said these words to me: "It dies to itself wholly, daughter, in order that it may fix itself more and more upon me; it is no longer itself that lives, but I. As it cannot comprehend what it understands, it is an understanding which understands not." One who has experienced this will understand something of it; it cannot be more clearly expressed, since all that comes to pass in this state is so obscure. I can only say that the soul feels close to God and that there abides within it such a certainty that it cannot possibly do other than believe. All the faculties now fail and are suspended in such a way that, as I have said, it is impossible to believe they are active. If the soul has been meditating upon any subject, this vanishes from its memory as if it had never thought of it. If it has been reading, it is unable to concentrate upon what it was reading or to remember it; and the same is true if it has been praying. So it is that this importunate little butterfly—the memory—is now burning its wings and can no longer fly.

Perfect Love

The will must be fully occupied in loving,
but it cannot understand how it loves; the
understanding, if it understands, does not
understand how it understands, or at least
can comprehend nothing of what it understands. It does not seem to me to be
understanding, because, as I say, it does not
understand itself. Nor can I myself understand this.

There was one thing of which at first I
was ignorant: I did not know that God was
in all things, and, when he seemed to me
to be so very present, I thought it impossible. I could not cease believing that he was
there, for it seemed almost certain that I
had been conscious of his very presence.
Unlearned persons would tell me that he
was there only by grace; but I could not
believe that, for, as I say, he seemed to me
to be really present; and so I continued to
be greatly distressed. From this doubt I was
freed by a very learned man of the Order

of the glorious Saint Dominic; he told me that he was indeed present and described how he communicated himself to us, which brought me very great comfort. It is to be noted and understood that this water from heaven, this greatest of the Lord's favors, leaves the greatest benefits in the soul.

PART II

The Way
of
Perfection

Teresa's main desire in writing The Way of Perfection *was to nurture her daughters in their love of prayer. For their instruction, she offers general guidelines for practice, themes for contemplation, and finally takes the reader through her own meditations on the Lord's Prayer, section by section. With Chapter 6 she takes up the subject of perfect love. Here she describes how one should approach God and others in prayer and in daily life, warning against expecting something in return for loving another. Chapter 7 continues with the same subject and includes her recommended methods for achieving perfect love. One type of prayer Teresa frequently speaks of in her writings, and which held great importance for her, is the Prayer of Quiet. In Chapter 31 she explains what this prayer is and how it can be employed to come closer to God.*

Chapter 6

I have digressed a great deal but no one will blame me who understands the importance of what has been said. Let us now return to the love which it is good and lawful for us to feel. This I have described as purely spiritual; I am not sure if I know what I am talking about, but it seems to me that there is no need to speak much of it, since so few, I fear, possess it; let any one of you to whom the Lord has given it praise him fervently, for she must be a person of the greatest perfection. It is about this that I now wish to write. Perhaps what I say may be of some profit, for if you look at a virtue you desire it and try to gain it, and so become attached to it.

Perfect Love

God grant that I may be able to understand this, and even more that I may be able to describe it, for I am not sure that I know when love is spiritual and when there is sensuality mingled with it, or how to begin speaking about it. I am like one who hears a person speaking in the distance and, *though he can hear that he is speaking,* cannot distinguish what he is saying. It is just like that with me; sometimes I cannot understand what I am saying, yet the Lord is pleased to enable me to say it well. If at other times what I say is ridiculous and nonsensical, it is only natural for me to go completely astray.

Now it seems to me that, when God has brought someone to a clear knowledge of the world, and of its nature, and of the fact that another world *(or, let us say, another kingdom)* exists, and that there is a great difference between the one and the other, the one being eternal and the other only a dream; and of what it is to love the creator and what to love the creature (this must be discovered by experience, for it is a very different matter from merely thinking about it and believing it); when one understands by sight and experience what can be gained by the one practice and lost by the other, and what the creator is and what the creature, and many other things which the Lord teaches to those who are willing to devote themselves to being taught by him in prayer, or whom his majesty wishes to teach—then one loves very differently from those of us who have not advanced thus far.

It may be, sisters, that you think it irrelevant for me to treat of this, and you may say that you already know everything that I have said. God grant that this may be so, and that you may indeed know it in the only way which has any meaning, and that it may be graven upon your inmost being, *and that you may never for a moment depart*

from it; for, if you know it, you will see that
I am telling nothing but the truth when I
say that he whom the Lord brings thus far
possesses this love. Those whom God
brings to this state are, *I think,* generous
and royal souls; they are not content with
loving anything so miserable as these bodies, however beautiful they be and however
numerous the graces they possess. If the
sight of the body gives them pleasure they
praise the creator, but as for dwelling upon
it *for more than just a moment*——no! When I
use that phrase "dwelling upon it," I refer
to having love for such things. If they had
such love, they would think they were loving something insubstantial and were
conceiving fondness for a shadow; they
would feel shame for themselves and would
not have the effrontery to tell God that
they love him, without feeling great confu-
sion.

You will answer me that such persons

cannot love or repay the affection shown to them by others. Certainly they care little about having this affection. They may from time to time experience a natural and momentary pleasure at being loved; yet, as soon as they return to their normal condition, they realize that such pleasure is folly save when the persons concerned can benefit their souls, either by instruction or by prayer. Any other kind of affection wearies them, for they know it can bring them no profit and may well do them harm; nonetheless they are grateful for it and recompense it by commending those who love them to God. They take this affection as something for which those who love them lay the responsibility upon the Lord, from whom, since they can see nothing lovable in themselves, they suppose the love comes, and think that others love them because God loves them; and so they leave his majesty to recompense them for this and beg him to do so, thus freeing themselves and feeling they have no more responsibility. When I ponder it carefully, I sometimes think this desire for affection is sheer blindness, except when, as I say, it relates to persons who can lead us to do good so that we may gain blessings in perfection.

It should be noted here that, when we desire anyone's affection, we always seek it because of some interest, profit or pleasure of our own. Those who are perfect, however, have trodden all these things beneath their feet—and have despised the blessings which may come to them in this world, and its pleasures and delights—in such a way that, even if they wanted to, so to say, they could not love anything outside God, or unless it had to do with God. What profit, then, can come to them from being loved themselves?

When this truth is put to them, they

The Way of Perfection

The Way of Perfection

laugh at the distress which had been assailing them in the past as to whether their affection was being returned or no. Of course, however pure our affection may be, it is quite natural for us to wish it to be returned. But, when we come to evaluate the return of affection, we realize that it is insubstantial, like a thing of straw, as light as air and easily carried away by the wind. For, however dearly we have been loved, what is there that remains to us? Such persons, then, except for the advantage that the affection may bring to their souls (because they realize that our nature is such that we soon tire of life without love), care nothing whether they are loved or not. Do you think that such persons will love none and delight in none save God? No; they will love others much more than they did, with a more genuine love, with greater passion and with a love which brings more profit; that, in a word, is what love really is. And such souls are always much fonder of giving than of receiving, even in their relations with the creator himself. This holy affection, I say, merits the name of love, which name has been usurped from it by those other base affections.

Do you ask, again, by what they are attracted if they do not love things they see? They do love what they see and they are greatly attracted by what they hear; but the things which they see are everlasting. If they love anyone they immediately look right beyond the body *(on which, as I say, they cannot dwell)*, fix their eyes on the soul and see what there is to be loved in that. If there is nothing, but they see any suggestion or inclination which shows them that, if they dig deep, they will find gold within this mine, they think nothing of the labor of digging, since they have love. There is nothing that suggests itself to them which they will not willingly do for the good of that soul since they desire their love for it to be lasting, and they know quite well that that is impossible unless the loved one has certain good qualities and a great love for God. I really mean that it is impossible, however great their obligations and even if that soul were to die for love of them and do them all the kind actions in its power; even had it all the natural graces joined in one, their wills would not have strength enough to love it nor would they remain fixed upon it. They know and have learned and experienced the worth of all this; no false dice can deceive them. They see that they are not in unison with that soul and that their love for it cannot possibly last; for, unless that soul keeps the law of God, their love will end with life—they know that unless it loves him they will go to different places.

Those into whose souls the Lord has already infused true wisdom do not esteem

this love, which lasts only on earth, at
more than its true worth—if, indeed, at so
much. Those who like to take pleasure in
worldly things, delights, honors and riches,
will account it of some worth if their friend
is rich and able to afford them pastime *and
pleasure* and recreation; but those who already hate all this will care little or nothing
for such things. If they have any love for
such a person, then, it will be a passion
that he may love God so as to be loved by
him; for, as I say, they know that no other
kind of affection but this can last, and that
this kind will cost them dear, for which
reason they do all they possibly can for
their friend's profit; they would lose a
thousand lives to bring him a small blessing. Oh, precious love, forever imitating
the Captain of Love, Jesus, our Good!

Chapter 7

It is strange to see how impassioned this love is; how many tears, penances and prayers it costs; how careful is the loving soul to commend the object of its affection to all who it thinks may prevail with God and to ask them to intercede with him for it; and how constant is its longing, so that it cannot be happy unless it sees that its loved one is making progress. If that soul seems to have advanced, and is then seen to fall some way back, her friend seems to have no more pleasure in life: she neither eats nor sleeps, is never free from this fear and is always afraid that the soul whom she loves so much may be lost, and that the two

may be parted forever. She cares nothing
for physical death, but she will not suffer
herself to be attached to something which a
puff of wind may carry away so that she is
unable to retain her hold upon it. This, as I
have said, is love without any degree what-
soever of self-interest; all that this soul
wishes and desires is to see the soul it loves
enriched with blessings from heaven. This
is love, quite unlike our ill-starred earthly
affections—to say nothing of illicit affections, from which may God keep us free.

These last affections are a very hell, and
it is needless for us to weary ourselves by
saying how evil they are, for the least of the
evils which they bring are terrible beyond
exaggeration. There is no need for us ever
to take such things upon our lips, sisters, *or
even to think of them,* or to remember that
they exist anywhere in the world; you must
never listen to anyone speaking of such affections, either in jest or in earnest, nor

allow them to be mentioned or discussed in your presence. No good can come from our doing this and it might do us harm even to hear them mentioned. But with regard to the lawful affections which, as I have said, we may have for each other, or for relatives and friends, it is different. Our whole desire is that they should not die: if their heads ache, our souls seem to ache too; if we see them in distress, we are unable (as people say) to sit still under it; and so on.

This is not so with spiritual affection. Although the weakness of our nature may at first allow us to feel something of all this, our reason soon begins to reflect whether our friend's trials are not good for her, and to wonder if they are making her richer in virtue and how she is bearing them, and then we shall ask God to give her patience so that they may win her merit. If we see that she is being patient, we feel no distress

—indeed, we are gladdened and consoled. If all the merit and gain which suffering is capable of producing could be made over to her, we should still prefer suffering her trial ourselves to seeing her suffer it, but we are not worried or disquieted.

I repeat once more that this love is a similitude and copy of that which was borne for us by the good lover, Jesus. It is for that reason that it brings us such immense benefits, for it makes us embrace every kind of suffering, so that others, without having to endure the suffering, may gain its advantages. The recipients of this friendship, then, profit greatly, but their friends should realize that either this intercourse—I mean, this exclusive friendship —must come to an end or that they must prevail upon our Lord that their friend may walk in the same way as themselves, as Saint Monica prevailed with him for Saint Augustine. Their heart does not allow them to practice duplicity: if they see their friend straying from the road, or committing any faults, they will speak to her about it; they cannot allow themselves to do anything else. And if after this the loved one does not amend, they will not flatter her or hide anything from her. Either, then, she will amend or their friendship will cease; for otherwise they would be unable to endure it, nor is it in fact endurable. It would mean continual war for both parties. A person may be indifferent to all other people in the world and not worry whether they are serving God or not, since the person she has to worry about is herself. But she cannot take this attitude with her friends. Nothing they do can be hidden from her; she sees the smallest mote in them. This, I repeat, is a very heavy cross for her to bear.

Happy the souls that are loved by such as these! Happy the day on which they came to

*know them! O my Lord, wilt thou not grant me
the favor of giving me many who have such love
for me? Truly, Lord, I would rather have this
than be loved by all the kings and lords of the
world—and rightly so, for such friends use every
means in their power to make us lords of the
whole world and to have all that is in it subject
to us. When you make the acquaintance of any
such persons, sisters, the Mother Prioress should
employ every possible effort to keep you in touch
with them. Love such persons as much as you
like. There can be very few of them, but nonetheless it is the Lord's will that their goodness
should be known. When one of you is striving
after perfection, she will at once be told that she
has no need to know such people—that it is
enough for her to have God. But to get to know
God's friends is a very good way of "having"
him; as I have discovered by experience, it is most
helpful. For, under the Lord, I owe it to such
persons that I am not in hell; I was always very*

*fond of asking them to commend me to God, and
so I prevailed upon them to do so.*

Let us now return to what we were saying. It
is this kind of love which I should like us to
have; at first it may not be perfect but the
Lord will make it increasingly so. Let us
begin with the methods of obtaining it. At
first it may be mingled with emotion, but
this, as a rule, will do no harm. It is sometimes good and necessary for us to show
emotion in our love, and also to feel it, and
to be distressed by some of our sisters' trials and weaknesses, however trivial they
may be. For on one occasion as much distress may be caused by quite a small matter
as would be caused on another by some
great trial, and there are people whose nature it is to be very much cast down by
small things. If you are not like this, do not
neglect to have compassion on others; it
may be that our Lord wishes to spare us
these sufferings and will give us sufferings

of another kind which will seem heavy to us, though to the person already mentioned they may seem light. In these matters, then, we must not judge others by ourselves, nor think of ourselves as we have been at some time when, perhaps without any effort on our part, the Lord has made us stronger than they; let us think of what we were like at the times when we have been weakest.

Note the importance of this advice for those of us who would learn to sympathize with our neighbors' trials, however trivial these may be. It is especially important for such souls as have been described, for, desiring trials as they do, they make light of them all. They must therefore try hard to recall what they were like when they were weak, and reflect that, if they are no longer so, it is not due to themselves. For otherwise, little by little, the devil could easily cool our charity toward our neighbors and make us think that what is really a failing on our part is perfection. In every respect we must be careful and alert, for the devil never slumbers. And the nearer we are to perfection, the more careful we must be, since his temptations are then much more cunning because there are no others that he dare send us; and if, as I say, we are not cautious, the harm is done before we realize it. In short, we must always watch and pray, for there is no better way than prayer of revealing these hidden wiles of the devil and making him declare his presence.

Contrive always, even if you do not care for it, to take part in your sisters' necessary recreation and to do so for the whole of the allotted time, for all considerate treatment of them is a part of perfect love. It is a very good thing for us to take compassion on each other's needs. See that you show no lack of discretion about things which are contrary to obedience. Though privately you may think the prioress' orders harsh ones, do not allow this to be noticed or tell anyone about it (except that you may speak of it, with all humility, to the prioress herself), for if you did so you would be doing a great deal of harm. Get to know what are the things in your sisters which you should be sorry to see and those about which you should sympathize with them; and always show your grief at any notorious fault which you may see in one of them. It is a good proof and test of our love if we can bear with such faults and not be shocked by them. Others, in their turn, will bear with your faults, which, if you include those of which you are not aware, must be much more numerous. Often commend to God any sister who is at fault and strive for your own part to practice the virtue which is the opposite of her fault with great perfection. Make determined efforts to do this so that you may teach your sister by your deeds what perhaps she could never learn by words nor gain by punishment.

The habit of performing some conspicuously virtuous action through seeing it performed by another is one which very easily takes root. This is good advice; do not forget it. Oh, how true and genuine will be the love of a sister who can bring profit to everyone by sacrificing her own profit to that of the rest! She will make a great advance in each of the virtues and keep her rule with great perfection.

• • • •

If one of you should be cross with another because of some hasty word, the matter must at once be put right and you must betake yourselves to earnest prayer. The same applies to the harboring of any grudge, or to party strife, or to the desire to be greatest, or to any nice point concerning your honor.

• • • •

Perfect Love

As this is so important I think I shall say a little more about it elsewhere, so I will not write at greater length here, *except to say that, provided they treat each other equally, I would rather that the nuns showed a tender and affectionate love and regard for each other, even though there is less perfection in this than in the love I have described, than that there were a single note of discord to be heard among them. May the Lord forbid this, for his own sake. Amen.*

Chapter 31

Now, daughters, I still want to describe this Prayer of Quiet to you, in the way I have heard it talked about, and as the Lord has been pleased to teach it to me, perhaps in order that I might describe it to you. It is in this kind of prayer, as I have said, that the Lord seems to me to begin to show us that he is hearing our petition; he begins to give us his kingdom on earth so that we may truly praise him and hallow his name and strive to make others do so likewise.

This is a supernatural state, and, however hard we try, we cannot reach it for ourselves; for it is a state in which the soul enters into peace, or rather in which the Lord gives it peace through his presence, as he did to that just man Simeon. In this state all the faculties are stilled. The soul, in a way which has nothing to do with the outward senses, realizes that it is now very close to its God, and that, if it were but a little closer, it would become one with him through union. This is not because it sees him either with its bodily or with its spiritual eyes. The just man Simeon saw no more than the glorious infant—a poor little child, who, to judge from the swaddling clothes in which he was wrapped and from the small number of the people whom he had *as a retinue* to take him up to the temple, might well have been the son of these poor people rather than the son of his heavenly father. But the child himself revealed to him who he was. Just so, though less clearly, does the soul know who he is. It cannot understand how it knows him, yet it sees that it is in the kingdom (or at least is near to the king who will give it the kingdom), and it feels such reverence that it dares to ask nothing. It is, as it were, in a swoon, both inwardly and outwardly, so that the outward man (let me call it the "body," and then you will understand me better) does not wish to move, but rests, like one who has almost reached the end of his journey, so that it may the better start again upon its way, with redoubled strength for its task.

The body experiences the greatest delight and the soul is conscious of a deep satisfaction. So glad is it merely to find itself near the fountain that, even before it has begun to drink, it has had its fill. There seems nothing left for it to desire. The faculties are stilled and have no wish to move, for any movement they may make appears to hinder the soul from loving God. They are not completely lost, however, since, two of them being free, they can realize in whose presence they are. It is the will that is in captivity now; and, if while in this state it is capable of experiencing any pain, the pain comes when it realizes that it will have to resume its liberty. The mind tries to occupy itself with only one thing, and the memory has no desire to busy itself with more; they both see that this is the one thing needful and that anything else will unsettle them. Persons in this state prefer the body to remain motionless, for otherwise their peace would be destroyed; for this reason they dare not stir. Speaking is a distress to them; they will spend a whole hour on a single repetition of the Paternoster. They are so close to God that they know they can make themselves understood by signs. They are in the palace, near to their king, and they see that he is already beginning to give them his kingdom on earth. *Sometimes tears come to their eyes,* but they weep very gently and quite without distress; their whole desire is the hallowing of this name. They seem not to be in the world, and have no wish to see or hear anything but their God; nothing distresses them, nor does it seem that anything can possibly do so. In short, for as long as this state lasts, they are so overwhelmed and absorbed by the joy and delight which they experience that they can think of nothing else to wish for, and will gladly say with Saint Peter: "Lord, let us make here three mansions."

Occasionally, during this Prayer of Quiet, God grants the soul another favor which is hard to understand if one has not had long experience of it. But any of you who have had this will at once recognize it and it will give you great comfort to know what it is. I believe God often grants this favor together with the other. When this quiet is felt in a high degree and lasts for a long time, I do not think that, if the will were not made fast to something, the peace could be of such long duration. Sometimes it goes on for a day, or for two days, and we find ourselves—I mean those who experience this state—full of this joy without understanding the reason. They see clearly that their whole self is not in what they are doing, but that the most important faculty is absent—namely, the will, which I think is united with its God—and that the other faculties are left free to busy themselves with his service. For this they have much more capacity at such a time, though when attending to worldly affairs they are dull and sometimes stupid.

It is a great favor which the Lord grants to these souls, for it unites the active life with the contemplative. At such times they serve the Lord in both these ways at once; the will, while in contemplation, is working without knowing how it does so; the other two faculties are serving him as

Martha did. Thus Martha and Mary work together. I know someone to whom the Lord often granted this favor; she could not understand it and asked a great contemplative about it; he told her that what she described was quite possible and had happened to himself. I think, therefore, that as the soul experiences such satisfaction in this Prayer of Quiet the will must be almost continuously united with him who alone can give it happiness.

I think it will be well, sisters, if I give some advice here to any of you whom the Lord, out of his goodness alone, has brought to this state, as I know that this has happened to some of you. First of all, when such persons experience this joy, without knowing whence it has come to them, but knowing at least that they could not have achieved it of themselves, they are tempted to imagine that they can prolong it and they may even try not to breathe. This is ridiculous; we can no more control this prayer than we can make the day break, or stop night from falling; it is supernatural and something we cannot acquire. The most we can do to prolong this favor is to realize that we can neither diminish nor add to it, but, being most unworthy and undeserving of it, can only receive it with thanksgiving. And we can best give thanks, not with many words, but by lifting up our eyes, like the publican.

It is well to seek greater solitude so as to make room for the Lord and allow his majesty to do his own work in us. The most we should do is occasionally, and quite gently, to utter a single word, like a person giving a little puff to a candle, when he sees it has almost gone out, so as to make it burn again; though, if it were fully alight, I suppose the only result of blowing it would be to put it out. I think the puff should be a gentle one because, if we begin to tax our brains by making up long speeches, the will may become active again.

Note carefully, friends, this piece of advice which I want to give you now. You will often find that these other two faculties are of no help to you. It may come about that the soul is enjoying the highest degree of quiet, and that the understanding has soared so far aloft that what is happening to it seems not to be going on in its own house at all; it *really* seems to be a guest in somebody else's house, looking for other lodgings, since its own lodging no longer satisfies it and it cannot remain there for long together. Perhaps this is only my own experience and other people do not find it so. But, speaking for myself, I sometimes long to die because I cannot cure this wandering of the mind. At other times the mind seems to be settled in its own abode and to be remaining there with the will as its companion. When all three faculties work together it is wonderful. The harmony is like that between husband and wife: if they are happy and love each other, both desire the same thing; but if the husband is unhappy in his marriage he soon begins to make the wife restless. Just so, when the will finds itself in this state of quiet, it must take no more notice of the understanding than it would of a madman, for, if it tries to draw the understanding along with it, it is bound to grow preoccupied and restless, with the result that this state of prayer will be all effort and no gain and the soul will lose what God has been giving it without any effort of its own.

Pay great attention to the following comparison, which *the Lord suggested to me when I was in this state of prayer, and which* seems to me very appropriate. The soul is like an infant still at its mother's breast; such is the mother's care for it that she gives it its milk without its having to ask for it so much as by moving its lips. That is what happens here. The will simply loves, and no effort needs to be made by the understanding, for it is the Lord's pleasure that, without exercising its thought, the soul should realize that it is in his company, and should merely drink the milk which his majesty puts into its mouth and enjoy its sweetness. The Lord desires it to know that it is he who is granting it that favor and that in its enjoyment of it he too rejoices. But it is not his will that the soul should try to understand how it is enjoying it, or what it is enjoying; it should lose all thought of itself, and he who is at its side will not fail to see what is best for it. If it begins to strive with its mind so that the mind may be apprised of what is happening and thus induced to share in it, it will be quite unable to do so, and the soul will perforce lose the milk and forgo that divine sustenance.

This state of prayer is different from that in which the soul is wholly united with God, for in the latter state it does not even swallow its nourishment; the Lord places this within it, and it has no idea how. But in this state it *even* seems to be his will that the soul should work a little, though so quietly that it is hardly conscious of doing so. What disturbs it is the understanding, and this is not the case when there is union of all the three faculties, since he who created them suspends them; he keeps them occupied with the enjoyment that he has given them, without their knowing, or being able to understand, the reason. *Anyone who has had experience of this kind of prayer will understand quite well what I am saying if, after reading this, she considers it carefully, and thinks out its meaning; otherwise it will be Greek to her.*

Well, as I say, the soul is conscious of having reached this state of prayer, which is a quiet, deep *and peaceful* happiness of the will, without being able to decide precisely what it is, although it can clearly see how it differs from the happiness of the world. To have dominion over the whole world, with all its happiness, would not suffice to bring the soul such inward satisfaction as it enjoys now in the depths of its will. For other kinds of happiness in life, it seems to me, touch only the outward part of the will, which we might describe as its rind.

When one of you finds herself in this sublime state of prayer, which, as I have already said, is most markedly supernatural, and the understanding (or, to put it more clearly, the thought) wanders off after the most ridiculous things in the world, she should laugh at it and treat it as the silly thing it is, and remain in her state of quiet. For thoughts will come and go, but the will is mistress and all-powerful, and will recall them without your having to trouble about it. But if you try to drag the understanding back by force, you lose your power over it, which comes from your taking and receiving that divine sustenance, and neither will nor understanding will gain, but both will be losers. There is a saying that, if we try very hard to grasp all, we lose all; and so I think it is here. Experience will show you the truth of this; and I shall not be surprised if those of you who have none think this very obscure and unnecessary. But, as I have said, if you have only a little experience of it you will understand it and be able to profit by it, and you will praise the Lord for being pleased to enable me to explain it.

Let us now conclude by saying that, when the soul is brought to this state of prayer, it would seem that the eternal father has already granted its petition that he will give it his kingdom on earth. O blessed request, in which we ask for so great a good without knowing what we do! Blessed manner of asking! It is for this reason, sisters, that I want us to be careful how we say this prayer, the Paternoster, and all other vocal prayers, *and what we ask for in them.* For *clearly,* when God has shown us this favor, we shall have to forget worldly things, all of which the Lord of the world has come and cast out. I do not mean that everyone who experiences the Prayer of Quiet must perforce be detached from everything in the world; but at least I should like all such persons to know what they lack and to humble themselves *and not to make so great a petition as though they were asking for nothing, and, if the Lord gives them what they ask for, to throw it back in his face.* They must try to become more and more detached from everything, for otherwise they will only remain where they are. If God gives a soul such pledges, it is a sign that he has great things in store for it. It will be its own fault if it does not make great progress. But if he sees that, after he has brought the kingdom of heaven into its abode, it returns to earth, not only will he refrain from showing it the secrets of his kingdom but he will grant it this other favor only for short periods and rarely.

I may be mistaken about this, but I have seen it and know that it happens, and, for my own part, I believe this is why spiritual people are not much more numerous. They do not respond to so great a favor in a practical way; instead of preparing themselves to receive this favor again, they take back from the Lord's hands the will which he considered his own and center it upon base things. So he seeks out others who love him in order to grant them his greater gifts, although he will not take away all that he has given from those who live in purity of conscience. But there are persons—and I have been one of them—to whom the Lord gives tenderness of devotion and holy inspirations and light on everything. He bestows this kingdom on them and brings them to this Prayer of Quiet, and yet they deafen their ears to his voice. For they are so fond of talking and of repeating a large number of vocal prayers in a great hurry, as though they were anxious to finish their task of repeating them daily, that when the Lord, as I say, puts his kingdom into their very hands, *by giving them this Prayer of Quiet and this inward peace,* they do not accept it, but think that they will do better to go on reciting their prayers, which only distract them from their purpose.

Do not be like that, sisters, but be watchful when the Lord grants you this favor. Think what a great treasure you may be losing and realize that you are doing much more by occasionally repeating a single petition of the Paternoster than by repeating the whole of it many times in a

hurry *and not thinking what you are saying.*
He to whom you are praying is very near to
you and will not fail to hear you; and you
may be sure that you are truly praising him
and hallowing his name, since you are glo-
rifying the Lord as a member of his
household and praising him with increasing
affection and desire so that it seems you can
never forsake his service. *So I advise you to
be very cautious about this, for it is of the greatest importance.*

PART III

The Interior Castle

The Interior Castle *is undoubtedly the most popular of Teresa's works and is regarded as one of the greatest works of mysticism ever written. Teresa, in contemplation for a treatise on prayer, saw in a vision the vehicle with which she could describe the experience of a soul journeying toward grace. In this vision, Teresa saw a beautiful crystal castle which was made up of seven mansions. Outside the castle everything was foul, dark, and hostile. But the closer one got to the seventh mansion at the center, the more intense was the light, splendor, and glory of God. Teresa begins this journey in the First Mansion, Chapter 1 dis-*

cussing the beauty and dignity of our souls. Understanding of this and all the gifts we receive from God comes through the door to this first mansion, which is prayer. Though close to the center, Chapter 7 of the Sixth Mansion shows how the journey does not get any easier the further along it goes. There are many difficulties for even those who have gotten this far, and Teresa reminds her students to keep in mind the humanity of Jesus himself through their trials and not to lose heart. Finally, in Chapter 4 of the Seventh Mansion, she tells us what seems to be God's intention in granting us such great gifts, and she uses Martha and Mary as examples for us to learn from.

FIRST MANSIONS

Chapter 1

Whi le I was beseeching our Lord to-
day that he would speak through
me, since I could find nothing to say and
had no idea how to begin to carry out the
obligation laid upon me by obedience, a
thought occurred to me which I will now
set down, in order to have some foundation
on which to build. I began to think of the
soul as if it were a castle made of a single
diamond or of very clear crystal, in which
there are many rooms, just as in heaven
there are many mansions. Now if we think

carefully over this, sisters, the soul of the righteous man is nothing but a paradise, in which, as God tells us, he takes his delight. For what do you think a room will be like which is the delight of a king so mighty, so wise, so pure and so full of all that is good? I can find nothing with which to compare the great beauty of a soul and its great capacity. In fact, however acute our intellects may be, they will no more be able to attain to a comprehension of this than to an understanding of God; for, as he himself says, he created us in his image and likeness. Now if this is so—and it is—there is no point in our fatiguing ourselves by attempting to comprehend the beauty of this castle; for, though it is his creature, and there is therefore as much difference between it and God as between creature and creator, the very fact that his majesty says it is made in his image means that we can hardly form any conception of the soul's great dignity and beauty.

It is no small pity, and should cause us no little shame, that, through our own fault, we do not understand ourselves, or know who we are. Would it not be a sign of great ignorance, my daughters, if a person were asked who he was, and could not say, and had no idea who his father or his mother was, or from what country he came? Though that is great stupidity, our own is incomparably greater if we make no attempt to discover what we are, and only know that we are living in these bodies, and have a vague idea, because we have heard it and because our faith tells us so, that we possess souls. As to what good qualities there may be in our souls, or who dwells within them, or how precious they are— those are things which we seldom consider and so we trouble little about carefully preserving the soul's beauty. All our interest is centered in the rough setting of the diamond, and in the outer wall of the castle—that is to say, in these bodies of ours.

Let us now imagine that this castle, as I have said, contains many mansions, some above, others below, others at each side; and in the center and midst of them all is the chiefest mansion where the most secret things pass between God and the soul. You must think over this comparison very carefully; perhaps God will be pleased to use it to show you something of the favors which he is pleased to grant to souls, and of the differences between them, so far as I have understood this to be possible, for there are so many of them that nobody can possibly understand them all, much less anyone as stupid as I. If the Lord grants you these favors, it will be a great consolation to you to know that such things are possible; and, if you never receive any, you can still praise his great goodness. For, as it does us no harm to think of the things laid up for us in heaven, and of the joys of the blessed, but rather makes us rejoice and strive to attain those joys ourselves, just so it will do us no harm to find that it is possible in this our exile for so great a God to commune with such malodorous worms, and to love him for his great goodness and boundless mercy. I am sure that anyone who finds it harmful to realize that it is possible for God to grant such favors during this our exile must be greatly lacking in humility and in love of his neighbor; for otherwise how could we help rejoicing that God should grant these favors to one of our brethren when this in no way hinders him from granting them to ourselves, and that his majesty should bestow an understanding of his greatness upon anyone soever? Sometimes he will do this only to manifest his power, as he said of the blind man to whom he gave his sight, when the apostles

asked him if he were suffering for his own
sins or for the sins of his parents. He grants
these favors, then, not because those who
receive them are holier than those who do
not, but in order that his greatness may be
made known, as we see in the case of Saint
Paul and the Magdalen, and in order that
we may praise him in his creatures.

It may be said that these things seem
impossible and that it is better not to scan-
dalize the weak. But less harm is done by
their disbelieving us than by our failing to
edify those to whom God grants these favors, and who will rejoice and will awaken
others to a fresh love of him who grants
such mercies, according to the greatness of
his power and majesty. In any case I know
that none to whom I am speaking will run
into this danger, because they all know and
believe that God grants still greater proofs
of his love. I am sure that, if any one of you
does not believe this, she will never learn it

by experience. For God's will is that no bounds should be set to his works. Never do such a thing, then, sisters, if the Lord does not lead you by this road.

Now let us return to our beautiful and delightful castle and see how we can enter it. I seem rather to be talking nonsense; for, if this castle is the soul, there can clearly be no question of our entering it. For we ourselves are the castle, and it would be absurd to tell someone to enter a room when he was in it already! But you must understand that there are many ways of "being" in a place. Many souls remain in the outer court of the castle, which is the place occupied by the guards; they are not interested in entering it, and have no idea what there is in that wonderful place, or who dwells in it, or even how many rooms it has. You will have read certain books on prayer which advise the soul to enter within itself; and that is exactly what this means.

A short time ago I was told by a very learned man that souls without prayer are like people whose bodies or limbs are paralyzed: they possess feet and hands but they cannot control them. In the same way, there are souls so infirm and so accustomed to busying themselves with outside affairs that nothing can be done for them, and it seems as though they are incapable of entering within themselves at all. So accustomed have they grown to living all the time with the reptiles and other creatures to be found in the outer court of the castle that they have almost become like them; and although by nature they are so richly endowed as to have the power of holding converse with none other than God himself, there is nothing that can be done for them. Unless they strive to realize their miserable condition and to remedy it, they will be turned into pillars of salt for not looking within themselves, just as Lot's wife was because she looked back.

As far as I can understand, the door of entry into this castle is prayer and meditation. I do not say mental prayer rather than vocal, for, if it is prayer at all, it must be accompanied by meditation. If a person does not think whom he is addressing, and what he is asking for, and who it is that is asking and of whom he is asking it, I do not consider that he is praying at all even though he be constantly moving his lips. True, it is sometimes possible to pray without paying heed to these things, but that is only because they have been thought about previously; if a man is in the habit of speaking to God's majesty as he would speak to his slave, and never wonders if he is expressing himself properly, but merely utters the words that come to his lips because he has learned them by heart through constant

repetition, I do not call that prayer at all—
and God grant no Christian may ever speak
to him so! At any rate, sisters, I hope in
God that none of you will, for we are accustomed here to talk about interior
matters, and that is a good way of keeping
oneself from falling into such animal-like
habits.

Let us say no more, then, of these paralyzed souls, who, unless the Lord himself
comes and commands them to rise, are like
the man who had lain beside the pool for
thirty years: they are unfortunate creatures
and live in great peril. Let us rather think
of certain other souls, who do eventually
enter the castle. These are very much absorbed in worldly affairs; but their desires
are good; sometimes, though infrequently,
they commend themselves to Our Lord;
and they think about the state of their
souls, though not very carefully. Full of a
thousand preoccupations as they are, they

pray only a few times a month, and as a rule they are thinking all the time of their preoccupations, for they are very much attached to them, and, where their treasure is, there is their heart also. From time to time, however, they shake their minds free of them and it is a great thing that they should know themselves well enough to realize that they are not going the right way to reach the castle door. Eventually they enter the first rooms on the lowest floor, but so many reptiles get in with them that they are unable to appreciate the beauty of the castle or to find any peace within it. Still, they have done a good deal by entering at all.

You will think this is beside the point, daughters, since by the goodness of the Lord you are not one of these. But you must be patient, for there is no other way in which I can explain to you some ideas I have had about certain interior matters

concerning prayer. May it please the
Lord to enable me to say something about
them; for to explain to you what I should
like is very difficult unless you have had
personal experience; and anyone with such
experience, as you will see, cannot help
touching upon subjects which, please God,
shall, by his mercy, never concern us.

SIXTH MANSIONS

Chapter 7

You will think, sisters, that these souls to whom the Lord communicates himself in so special a way (I am speaking now particularly to those who have not attained these favors, for if they have been granted the enjoyment of such favors by God, they will know what I am about to say) will by now be so sure that they are to enjoy him forever that they will have no reason to fear or to weep for their sins. This will be a very great mistake, for, the more they receive from our God, the

greater grows their sorrow for sin; I believe
myself that this will never leave us until we
reach that place where nothing can cause us
affliction.

It is true that this sorrow can be more
oppressive at one time than at another, and
also that it is of different kinds; for the soul
does not now think of the pain which it is
bound to suffer on account of its sins, but
only of how ungrateful it has been to him
whom it owes so much, and who so greatly
merits our service. For through these mani-
festations of his greatness which he
communicates to it the soul gains a much
deeper knowledge of the greatness of God.
It is aghast at having been so bold; it weeps
for its lack of reverence; its foolish mistakes
in the past seem to it to have been so gross
that it cannot stop grieving, when it re-
members that it forsook so great a majesty
for things so base. It thinks of this much
more than of the favors it receives, great as

they are like those which we have described and like those which remain to be described later. It is as if a mighty river were running through the soul and from time to time bringing these favors with it. But its sins are like the river's slimy bed; they are always fresh in its memory; and this is a heavy cross to it.

I know of a person who had ceased wishing she might die so as to see God, but was desiring death in order that she might not suffer such constant distress at the thought of her ingratitude to one to whom her debts were so great. She thought nobody's evil deeds could equal hers, for she believed there was no one with whom God had borne for so long and to whom he had shown so many favors.

• • • •

However favored by God a soul may be, I should not think it secure were it to forget the miserable state it was once in, for, distressing though the reflection is, it is often profitable. Perhaps it is because I myself have been so wicked that I feel like this and for that reason always keep it in mind; those who have been good will have nothing to grieve for, although for as long as we live in this mortal body we shall always have failures. It affords us no relief from this distress to reflect that our Lord has forgiven and forgotten our sins; in fact the thought of so much goodness and of favors granted to one who has merited only hell makes the distress greater. I think these reflections must have been a regular martyrdom for Saint Peter and for the Magdalen; because, as their love was so great and they had received so many favors and had learned to understand the greatness and majesty of God, they would find them terribly hard to bear, and must have been moved with the deepest emotion.

You will also think that anyone who enjoys such sublime favors will not engage in meditation on the most sacred humanity of our Lord Jesus Christ, because by that time he will be wholly proficient in love. This is a thing of which I have written at length elsewhere, and, although I have been contradicted about it and told that I do not understand it, because these are paths along which our Lord leads us, and that, when we have got over the first stages, we shall do better to occupy ourselves with matters concerning the godhead and to flee from corporeal things, they will certainly not make me admit that this is a good way. I may be wrong and we may all be meaning the same thing; but it was clear to me that the devil was trying to deceive me in this way; and I have had to learn my lesson. So, although I have often spoken about this, I propose to speak to you about it again, so that you may walk very warily.

• • • •

Perfect Love

Some souls also imagine that they cannot dwell upon the passion, in which case they will be able still less to meditate upon the most sacred virgin and the lives of the saints, the remembrance of whom brings us such great profit and encouragement. I cannot conceive what they are thinking of; for, though angelic spirits, freed from everything corporeal, may remain permanently enkindled in love, this is not possible for those of us who live in this mortal body. We need to cultivate, and think upon, and seek the companionship of those who, though living on earth like ourselves, have accomplished such great deeds for God; the last thing we should do is to withdraw of set purpose from our greatest help and blessing, which is the most sacred humanity of our Lord Jesus Christ. I cannot believe that people can really do this; it must be that they do not understand themselves and thus do harm to themselves and to others.

At any rate, I can assure them that they will not enter these last two mansions; for, if they lose their guide, the good Jesus, they will be unable to find their way; they will do well if they are able to remain securely in the other mansions. For the Lord himself says that he is the way; the Lord also says that he is light and that no one can come to the father save by him; and "he that seeth me seeth my father." It may be said that these words have another meaning. I do not know of any such meaning myself; I have got on very well with the meaning which my soul always feels to be the true one.

There are some people (and a great many of them have spoken to me about this) on whom our Lord bestows perfect contemplation and who would like to remain in possession of it forever. That is impossible; but they retain something of this divine favor, with the result that they can no longer meditate upon the mysteries of the passion and the life of Christ, as they could before. I do not know the reason for this, but it is quite a common experience in such cases for the understanding to be less apt for meditation. I think the reason must be that the whole aim of meditation is to seek God, and once he is found, and the soul grows accustomed to seeking him again by means of the will, it has no desire to fatigue itself with intellectual labor. It also seems to me that, as the will is now enkindled, this generous faculty would have no desire to make use of that other faculty, even if it could. There would be nothing wrong in its setting it aside, but it is impossible for it to do so, especially before the soul has reached these last mansions, and it will only lose time by attempting it, for the aid of the understanding is often needed for the enkindling of the will.

Note this point, sisters, for it is important, so I will explain it further. The soul is desirous of employing itself wholly in love and it would be glad if it could meditate on nothing else. But this it cannot do even if it so desires; for, though the will is not dead, the fire which habitually kindles it is going out, and, if it is to give off heat of itself, it needs someone to fan it into flame. Would it be a good thing for the soul to remain in that state of aridity, hoping for fire to come down from heaven to burn up this sacrifice of itself which it is making to God as did our father Elias? No, certainly not; nor is it a good thing to expect miracles; the Lord will perform them for this soul when he sees fit to do so, as has been said and as will be said again later. But his majesty wants us to realize our wickedness, which makes us unworthy of their being wrought, and to do everything we possibly can to come to our own aid. And I believe myself that, however sublime our prayer may be, we shall have to do this until we die.

It is true that anyone whom our Lord brings to the seventh mansion very rarely, or never, needs to engage in this activity, for the reason that I shall set down, if I remember to do so, when I come to deal with that mansion, where in a wonderful way the soul never ceases to walk with Christ our Lord but is ever in the company of both his divine and his human nature. When, therefore, the aforementioned fire is not kindled in the will, and the presence of God is not felt, we must needs seek it, since this is his majesty's desire, as the bride sought it in the *Songs*. Let us ask the creatures who made them, as Saint Augustine says that he did (in his *Meditations* or *Confessions,* I think) and let us not be so foolish as to lose time by waiting to receive what has been given us once already. At first it may be that the Lord will not give it us, for as long as a year, or even for many years; his majesty knows why; it is not our business to want to know, nor is there any reason why we should. Since we know the way we have to take to please God—namely, that of keeping his commandments and counsels—let us be very diligent in doing this, and in meditating upon his life and death, and upon all that we owe him; and let the rest come when the Lord wills.

Such people will reply that they cannot stop to meditate upon these things, and here they may to some extent be right, for the reason already given. You know, of course, that it is one thing to reason with the understanding and quite another for the memory to represent truths to the understanding. You will say, perhaps, that you do not understand me, and it may very well be that I do not understand the matter myself sufficiently to be able to explain it; but I will deal with it as well as I can. By meditation I mean prolonged reasoning with the understanding, in this way. We begin by thinking of the favor which God bestowed upon us by giving us his only son; and we do not stop there but proceed to consider the mysteries of his whole glorious life. Or we begin with the prayer in the garden and go on rehearsing the events that follow until we come to the crucifixion. Or we take one episode of the passion—Christ's arrest, let us say—and go over this mystery in our mind, meditating in detail upon the points in it which we need to think over and to try to realize, such as the treason of Judas, the flight of the Apostles, and so on. This is an admirable and a most meritorious kind of prayer.

This is the kind of prayer I was referring to which those whom God has raised to supernatural things and to perfect contemplation are right in saying they cannot practice. As I have said, I do not know why this should be the case; but as a rule they are in fact unable to do so. A man will not be right, however, to say that he cannot dwell upon these mysteries, for he often has them in his mind, especially when they are being celebrated by the Catholic Church; nor is it possible that a soul which has received so much from God should forget all these precious signs of his love, for they are living sparks which will enkindle the soul more and more in its love for our Lord. But these mysteries will not be apprehended by the understanding; the soul will understand them in a more perfect way. First, the understanding will picture them to itself, and then they will be impressed upon the memory, so that the mere sight of the Lord on his knees, in the garden, covered with that terrible sweat, will suffice us, not merely for an hour, but for many days. We consider, with a simple regard, who he is and how ungrateful we have been to one who has borne such pain for us. Then the will is aroused, not perhaps with deep emotion but with a desire to make some kind of return for this great favor, and to suffer something for one who has suffered so much himself. And so it is with other subjects, in which both memory and understanding will have a place. This, I think, is why the soul cannot reason properly about the passion, and it is because of this that it believes itself unable to meditate upon it at all.

But if it does not already meditate in this way, it will be well advised to attempt to do so; for I know that the most sublime kind of prayer will be no obstacle to it and I believe omission to practice it often would be a great mistake. If while the soul is meditating the Lord should suspend it, well and good; for in that case he will make it cease meditation even against its own will. I consider it quite certain that this method of procedure is no hindrance to the soul but a great help to it in everything that is good;

whereas, if it labored hard at meditation in the way I have already described, this would indeed be a hindrance—in fact, I believe such labor is impossible for a person who has attained greater heights. This may not be so with everyone, since God leads souls by many ways, but those who are unable to take this road should not be condemned or judged incapable of enjoying the great blessings contained in the mysteries of Jesus Christ our good. No one, however spiritual, will persuade me that to neglect these mysteries can be profitable for him.

Some souls, at the beginning of the spiritual life, or even when well advanced in it, get as far as the Prayer of Quiet, and are about to enjoy the favors and consolations given by the Lord in that state, and then think it would be a very great thing to be enjoying these gifts all the time. Let them take my advice, and become less absorbed in them, as I have said elsewhere. For life is long and there are many trials in it and we have need to look at Christ our pattern, and also at his apostles and saints, and to reflect how they bore these trials, so that we, too, may bear them perfectly. The good Jesus is too good company for us to forsake him and his most sacred mother. He is very glad when we grieve for his afflictions although sometimes we may be forsaking our own pleasures and consolations in order to do so—though for that matter, daughters, consolations in prayer are not so frequent that there is not time for everything. If anyone told me that she experienced them continuously (I mean so continuously that she could never meditate in the way I have described) I should consider it suspicious. Keep on with your meditation, then, and endeavor to be free from this error, and make every effort to avoid this absorption. If your efforts are not sufficient, tell the prioress, in order that she may give you some work which will keep you so busy that this danger will no longer exist. Any continuous exposure to it would be very bad for the brain and the head, if nothing worse.

I think I have explained what it is well for you to know—namely that, however spiritual you are, you must not flee so completely from corporeal things as to think that meditation on the most sacred humanity can actually harm you.

• • • •

The mistake, I think, which I used to make was only that I would take less pleasure than previously in thinking of our Lord Jesus Christ and would go about in that state of absorption, expecting to receive spiritual consolation. Then I saw clearly that I was going wrong; for, as it was impossible always to be having consolations, my thoughts would keep passing from one subject to another, until my soul, I think, got like a bird flying round and round in search of a resting place and losing a great deal of time, without advancing in the virtues or making progress in prayer. I could not understand the cause—nor, I believe, should I ever have understood it, because I thought I was on the proper road—until one day, when I was telling a person who was a servant of God about my method of prayer, he gave me some counsel. This showed me clearly how far I had gone astray and I have never ceased regretting that there was once a time when I failed to realize that so great a loss could not possibly result in gain. Even if I could obtain it, I want no blessing save that which I acquire through him by whom all blessings come to us. May he be praised forever. Amen.

SEVENTH MANSIONS

Chapter 4

You must not take it, sisters, that the
effects which I have described as oc-
curring in these souls are invariably present
all the time; it is for this reason that, whenever I have remembered to do so, I have
referred to them as being present "habitually." Sometimes our Lord leaves such
souls to their own nature, and when that
happens, all the poisonous things in the en-
virons and mansions of this castle seem to
come together to avenge themselves on
them for the time during which they have
not been able to have them in their power.

Perfect Love

It is true that this lasts only for a short time—for a single day, or a little longer, at the most—and in the course of the ensuing turmoil, which as a rule is the result of some chance happening, it becomes clear what the soul is gaining from the good companion who is with it. For the Lord gives it great determination, so that it will on no account turn aside from his service and from its own good resolutions. On the contrary, these resolutions seem to increase, and so the soul will not make the slightest move which may deflect it from its resolve. This, as I say, happens rarely, but our Lord's will is for the soul not to forget what it is—for one reason, so that it may always be humble; for another, so that it may the better realize what it owes to his majesty and what a great favor it is receiving, and may praise him.

Do not, of course, for one moment imagine that, because these souls have such vehement desires and are so determined not to commit a single imperfection for anything in the world, they do not in fact commit many imperfections, and even sins. Not intentionally, it is true, for the Lord will give such persons very special aid as to this. I am referring to venial sins, for from mortal sins, as far as they know, they are free, though they are not completely proof against them; and the thought that they may commit some without knowing it will cause them no small agony. It also distresses them to see so many souls being lost; and, although on the one hand they have great hopes of not being among them, yet, when they remember some whom the scriptures describe as having been favored of the Lord —like Solomon, who enjoyed such converse with his majesty—they cannot, as I have said, but be afraid. And let whichever of you feels surest of herself fear most, for, says David, "Blessed is the man that feareth

God." May his majesty always protect us; let us beseech him to do so, that we may not offend him; this is the greatest security that we can have. May he be forever praised. Amen.

It will be a good thing, sisters, if I tell you why it is that the Lord grants so many favors in this world. Although you will have learned this from the effects they produce, if you have observed them, I will speak about it further here, so that none of you shall think that he does it simply to give these souls pleasure. That would be to make a great error. For his majesty can do nothing greater for us than grant us a life which is an imitation of that lived by his beloved son. I feel certain, therefore, that these favors are given us to strengthen our weakness, as I have sometimes said here, so that we may be able to imitate him in his great sufferings.

We always find that those who walked

closest to Christ our Lord were those who had to bear the greatest trials. Consider the trials suffered by his glorious mother and by the glorious apostles. How do you suppose Saint Paul could endure such terrible trials? We can see in his life the effects of genuine visions and of contemplation coming from our Lord and not from human imagination or from the deceit of the devil. Do you imagine that he shut himself up with his visions so as to enjoy those divine favors and pursue no other occupation? You know very well that, so far as we can learn, he took not a day's rest, nor can he have rested by night, since it was then that he had to earn his living. I am very fond of the story of how, when Saint Peter was fleeing from prison, our Lord appeared to him and told him to go back to Rome and be crucified. We never recite the Office on his festival, in which this story is found, without my deriving a special consolation from it. How did Saint Peter feel after receiving this favor from the Lord? And what did he do? He went straight to his death; and the Lord showed him no small mercy in providing someone to kill him.

Oh, my sisters, how little one should think about resting, and how little one should care about honors, and how far one ought to be from wishing to be esteemed in the very least if the Lord makes his special abode in the soul. For if the soul is much with him, as it is right it should be, it will very seldom think of itself; its whole thought will be concentrated upon finding ways to please him and upon showing him how it loves him. This, my daughters, is the aim of prayer; this is the purpose of the spiritual marriage, of which are born good works and good works alone.

Such works, as I have told you, are the sign of every genuine favor and of everything else that comes from God. It will profit me little if I am alone and deeply recollected, and make acts of love to our Lord and plan and promise to work wonders in his service, and then, as soon as I leave my retreat and some occasion presents itself, I do just the opposite. I was wrong when I said it will profit me little, for anyone who is with God must profit greatly, and, although after making these resolutions we may be too weak to carry them out, his majesty will sometimes grant us grace to do so, even at great cost to ourselves, as often happens. For, when he sees a very timorous soul, he sends it, much against its own will, some very sore trial the bearing of which does it a great deal of good; and later, when the soul becomes aware of this, it loses its fear and offers itself to him the more readily. What I meant was that the profit is small by comparison with the far greater profit which comes from conformity between our deeds on the one hand and our resolutions and the words we use on the other. Anyone who cannot achieve everything at once must progress little by little. If she wishes to find help in prayer, she must learn to subdue her own will and in these little nooks of ours there will be very many occasions when you can do this.

Reflect carefully on this, for it is so important that I can hardly lay too much stress on it. Fix your eyes on the crucified and nothing else will be of much importance to you. If his majesty revealed his love to us by doing and suffering such amazing things, how can you expect to please him by words alone? Do you know when people really become spiritual? It is when they become the slaves of God and are branded with his sign, which is the sign of the cross, in token that they have given him their freedom. Then he can sell them as slaves to the whole world, as he himself

was sold, and if he does this he will be
doing them no wrong but showing them no
slight favor. Unless they resolve to do this,
they need not expect to make great progress. For the foundation of this whole
edifice, as I have said, is humility, and, if
you have not true humility, the Lord will
not wish it to reach any great height; in
fact, it is for your own good that it should
not; if it did, it would fall to the ground.
Therefore, sisters, if you wish to lay good
foundations, each of you must try to be the
least of all, and the slave of God, and must
seek a way and means to please and serve
all your companions. If you do that, it will
be of more value to you than to them and
your foundation will be so firmly laid that
your castle will not fall.

I repeat that if you have this in view you
must not build upon foundations of prayer
and contemplation alone, for, unless you
strive after the virtues and practice them,

you will never grow to be more than dwarfs. God grant that nothing worse than this may happen—for, as you know, anyone who fails to go forward begins to go back, and love, I believe, can never be content to stay for long where it is.

You may think that I am speaking about beginners, and that later on one may rest: but, as I have already told you, the only repose that these souls enjoy is of an interior kind; of outward repose they get less and less, and they have no wish to get more. What is the purpose, do you suppose, of these inspirations—or, more correctly, of these aspirations—which I have described, and of these messages which are sent by the soul from its innermost center to the folk outside the castle and to the mansions which are outside that in which it is itself dwelling? Is it to send them to sleep? No, no, no. The soul, where it now is, is fighting harder to keep the faculties and senses and everything to do with the body from being idle than it did when it suffered with them. For it did not then understand what great gain can be derived from trials, which may indeed have been means whereby God has brought it to this state, nor did it realize how the companionship which it now enjoys would give it much greater strength than it ever had before. For if, as David says, with the holy we shall be holy, it cannot be doubted that, if we are made one with the strong, we shall gain strength through the most sovereign union of spirit with spirit, and we shall appreciate the strength of the saints which enabled them to suffer and die.

It is quite certain that, with the strength it has gained, the soul comes to the help of all who are in the castle, and, indeed, succors the body itself. Often the body appears to feel nothing, but the strength derived from the vigor gained by the soul after it has drunk of the wine from this cellar, where its spouse has brought it and which he will not allow it to leave, overflows into the weak body, just as on the earthly plane the food which is introduced into the stomach gives strength to the head and to the whole body. In this life, then, the soul has a very bad time, for, however much it accomplishes, it is strong enough inwardly to attempt much more and this causes such strife within it that nothing it can do seems to it of any importance. This must be the reason for the great penances done by many saints, especially by the glorious Magdalen, who had been brought up in such luxury all her life long; there was also that hunger for the honor of his God suffered by our father Elias; and the zeal of Saint Dominic and Saint Francis for bringing souls to God, so that he might be praised. I assure you that, forgetful as they were of themselves, they must have endured no little suffering.

This, my sisters, I should like us to strive to attain: we should desire and engage in prayer, not for our enjoyment, but for the sake of acquiring this strength which fits us for service. Let us not try to walk along an untrodden path, or at the best we shall waste our time; it would certainly be a novel idea to think of receiving these favors from God through any other means than those used by him and by all his saints. Let us not even consider such a thing; believe me, Martha and Mary must work together when they offer the Lord lodging, and must have him ever with them, and they must not entertain him badly and give him nothing to eat. And how can Mary give him anything, seated as she is at his feet, unless her sister helps her? His food consists in our bringing him souls, in every possible way, so that they may be saved and may praise him forever.

You will reply to me by making two observations. The first, that Mary was said to have chosen the better part—and she had already done the work of Martha and shown her love for the Lord by washing his feet and wiping them with her hair. And do you think it would be a trifling mortification to a woman in her position to go through those streets—perhaps alone, for her fervor was such that she cared nothing how she went—to enter a house that she had never entered before and then to have to put up with uncharitable talk from the Pharisee and from very many other people, all of which she was forced to endure? What a sight it must have been in the town to see such a woman as she had been making this change in her life! Such people would only need to see that she was friendly with the Lord, whom they so bitterly hated, to call to mind the life which she had lived and to realize that she now wanted to become holy, for she would of course at once have changed her style of dress and everything else. Think how we gossip about people far less notorious than she and then imagine what she must have suffered. I assure you, sisters, that that better part came to her only after sore trials and great mortification—even to see her master so much hated must have been an intolerable trial to her. And how many such trials did she not endure later, after the Lord's death! The later years of her life, too, during which she was absent from him, would have been years of terrible torment; so she was not always enjoying the delights of contemplation at the Lord's feet.

The other thing you may say is that you are unable to lead souls to God, and have no means of doing so; that you would gladly do this, but, being unable to teach and preach like the apostles, you do not know how. That is an objection which I have often answered in writing, though I am not sure if I have done so in discussing this castle. But, as it is a thing which I think must occur to you, in view of the desires which the Lord implants in you, I will not omit to speak of it here. I told you elsewhere that the devil sometimes puts ambitious desires into our hearts, so that, instead of setting our hand to the work which lies nearest to us, and thus serving our Lord in ways within our power, we may rest content with having desired the impossible. Apart from praying for people, by which you can do a great deal for them, do not try to help everybody, but limit yourselves to your own companions; your work will then be all the more effective because you have the greater obligation to do it. Do you imagine it is a small advantage that you should have so much humility and mortification, and should be the servants of all and show such great charity toward all, and such fervent love for the Lord that it resembles a fire kindling all their souls, while you constantly awaken their zeal by your other virtues? This would indeed be a great service to the Lord and one very pleasing to him. By your doing things which you really can do, his majesty will know that you would like to do many more, and thus he will reward you exactly as if you had won many souls for him.

"But we shall not be converting anyone," you will say, "for all our sisters are good already." What has that to do with it? If they become still better, their praises will be more pleasing to the Lord, and their prayers of greater value to their neighbors. In a word, my sisters, I will end by saying that we must not build towers without foundations, and that the Lord does not look so much at the magnitude of anything we do as at the love with which we do it. If we accomplish what we can, his majesty will see to it that we become able to do more each day. We must not begin by growing weary; but during the whole of this short life, which for any one of you may be shorter than you think, we must offer the Lord whatever interior and exterior sacrifice we are able to give him, and his majesty will unite it with that which he offered to the father for us upon the cross, so that it may have the value won for it by our will, even though our actions in themselves may be trivial.

May it please his majesty, my sisters and daughters, to bring us all to meet where we may praise him and to give me grace to do some of the things of which I have told you, through the merits of his son, who liveth and reigneth forever, Amen. As I say this to you I am full of shame and by the same Lord I beg you not to forget this poor miserable creature in your prayers.

PART IV

Maxims

In addition to her full-length works, Teresa also set down many short words of wisdom as reminders to the sisters under her direction. Some specifically addressed the needs of cloistered living, but most (including those following) were valuable directives which can be helpful to anyone seeking a spiritual life.

—⚭—

Untilled soil, however fertile it may be, will bear thistles and thorns; and so it is with man's mind.

—⚭—

When you are with many people, always say little.

—⚭—

Be modest in all you do and in all your intercourse with others.

—⚭—

Never be importunate, especially about things of little moment.

—⚬—

Accustom yourself continually to make many acts of love, for they enkindle and melt the soul.

—⚬—

Speak to everyone with restrained cheerfulness.

—⚬—

Never reprove anyone save discreetly, humbly, and with a sense of your own shame.

—⚬—

Fall in with the mood of the person to whom you are speaking. Be happy with those who are happy and sad with those who are sad. In a word, be all things to all men so that you may gain all men.

—∿—

Never speak of anything concerning your-self which is worthy of praise—such as your learning, virtues, or descent—unless with the hope that some profit will come of it. If you do so speak, let it be with humil-ity, and the remembrance that these are gifts from the hand of God.

—∿—

Never exaggerate, but express your feelings with moderation.

—∿—

Never affirm anything unless you are sure it is true.

—∿—

Never thrust yourself forward and give your opinion about anything unless you are asked for it, or charity requires that you should give it.

—⚬—

If anyone is speaking of spiritual matters, listen to him humbly, as a learner, and apply to yourself all the good things you hear.

—⚬—

Do not eat or drink, save at the proper times, and then give hearty thanks to God.

—⚬—

Do everything as though you really saw his majesty before you; by acting thus a soul gains greatly.

—⚬—

Listen to ill of no one and speak ill of no one save of yourself; when you begin to like doing this, you are making good progress.

—∞—

Address every action that you perform to God; offer it to him and beg him that it may be to his honor and glory.

—∞—

When you are joyful, do not express your joy by laughing overmuch, but let it be humble, modest, pleasant, and edifying.

—∞—

Always think of yourself as everyone's servant; look for Christ our Lord in everyone and you will then have respect and reverence for all.

—∞—

In all you do and at all times examine your conscience, and, having seen your faults, strive with divine help to amend them; by following this course you will attain perfection.

—⚈—

Think not of the faults of others but of their virtues and of your own faults.

—⚈—

Always avoid being singular, as far as you can, for in community life this is a great evil.

—⚈—

Never do anything which you could not do in the sight of all.

—⚈—

Keep in mind your past life, so that you may bewail it, and likewise your present lukewarmness, and the distance you have still to go before you reach heaven; you will then live in fear, which is a source of great blessings.

—☙—

Never compare one person with another; comparisons are odious.

—☙—

Be gentle to all and stern with yourself.

—☙—

When reproved for anything, receive the reproof with both outward and inward humility, and pray to God for the person who has given it you.

—☙—

Remember that you have only one soul; that you have only one death to die; that you have only one life, which is short and has to be lived by you alone; and that there is only one glory, which is eternal. If you do this, there will be many things about which you care nothing.

Let your desire be to see God; your fear, that you may lose him; your sorrow, that you are not having fruition of him; your joy, that he can bring you to himself. Thus you will live in great peace.